To:

....

From:

....

Date:

....

THE
Lord Bless
YOU AND KEEP YOU

A Treasury of
GOD'S PROMISES

Pi Pocket
INSPIRATIONS

...inspired by life

© 2011 Ellie Claire™ Gift & Paper Corp.
a division of Worthy Media, Inc.
Brentwood, TN 37207
www.ellieclaire.com

THE LORD BLESS YOU AND KEEP YOU

A Treasury of God's Promises

ISBN 978-1-60936-246-1

Scripture references are from the following sources: The Holy Bible,
New International Version®, NIV®. Copyright © 1973, 1978, 1984, 2011
by Biblica, Inc.™ Used by permission of Zondervan. All rights reserved
worldwide. The Holy Bible, English Standard Version® (ESV),
copyright © 2001 by Crossway Bibles, a publishing ministry of Good
News Publishers. Used by permission. The New American Standard
Bible® (NASB), Copyright © 1960, 1962, 1963, 1968, 1971, 1972, 1973,
1975, 1977, 1995 by The Lockman Foundation. Used by permission.
The Holy Bible, New Living Translation (NLT), copyright 1996, 2004,
2007. Used by permission of Tyndale House Publishers, Inc., Carol
Stream, Illinois 60188. *The Message* (MSG). Copyright © 1993, 1994, 1995,
1996, 2000, 2001, 2002 by Eugene Peterson. Used by permission of
NavPress, Colorado Springs, CO. *The Living Bible* (TLB) © 1971. Used by
permission of Tyndale House Publishers, Inc., Carol Stream, Illinois
60188. The New Century Version® (NCV). Copyright © 1987, 1988, 1991,
2005 by Thomas Nelson, Inc. Used by permission. All rights reserved.

Excluding Scripture verses and divine pronouns, in some quotations
references to men and masculine pronouns have been replaced with
gender-neutral or feminine references.

Stock or custom editions of Ellie Claire titles may be purchased in bulk for
educational, business, ministry, fundraising, or sales promotional use. For
information, please e-mail info@ellieclaire.com.

Compiled by Joanie Garborg and Barbara Farmer
Cover and interior design by Jenny Bethke

Printed in USA.

CONTENTS

The greatest blessing of all is to
awaken to the understanding of God's love.
Our hearts fill and we overflow with that love,
spilling it and splashing it all around until
it becomes a blessing to all.

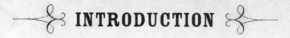

INTRODUCTION

God delivers His blessings to us, His children,
in so many different ways. It could be sunshine;
it could be rain. The gifts He gives are always
just what we need, for He knows our every need
better than we do. The blessings not only cheer,
but heal and guide and comfort.

The Lord Bless You and Keep You is a collection
of Scripture, words from God that He wants you
to know. Quotations—filled with encouragement,
grace, and love—complement each themed
message. Let the sacred passages and uplifting
quotations meet you right where you are,
touching your heart and soul.

May the blessings of the Lord be present
in your life, both now and always.

BLESSINGS TO EMBRACE

Does not wisdom call?...
"Take my instruction instead of silver,
and knowledge rather than choice gold,
for wisdom is better than jewels,
and all that you may desire
cannot compare with her....
Blessed are those who keep my ways.
Hear instruction and be wise,
and do not neglect it.
Blessed is the one who listens to me,
watching daily at my gates.
For whoever finds me finds life
and obtains favor from the LORD."

PROVERBS 8:1, 10-11, 32-35 ESV

The LORD longs to be gracious to you...
he will rise up to show you compassion.

ISAIAH 30:18 NIV

May the Lord direct your hearts
into God's love and Christ's perseverance....
Now may the Lord of peace himself
give you peace at all times and
in every way. The Lord be with all of you....
The grace of our Lord Jesus Christ
be with you all.

2 THESSALONIANS 3:5, 16, 18 NIV

*God's will is determined by
His wisdom which always
perceives, and His goodness
which always embraces,
the intrinsically good.*

— *C. S. Lewis* —

STEADFAST LOVE

This I call to mind,
and therefore I have hope:
The steadfast love of the LORD never ceases;
his mercies never come to an end;
they are new every morning;
great is your faithfulness.
"The LORD is my portion," says my soul,
"therefore I will hope in him."
The LORD is good to those who wait for him,
to the soul who seeks him.

LAMENTATIONS 3:21-25 ESV

Know therefore that the LORD your God is God;
he is the faithful God, keeping his covenant
of love to a thousand generations of those
who love him and keep his commandments.

DEUTERONOMY 7:9 NIV

You, Lord, are a compassionate
and gracious God, slow to anger,
abounding in love and faithfulness.

PSALM 86:15 NIV

It is good to give thanks to the LORD
And to sing praises to Your name, O Most High;
To declare Your lovingkindness in the morning
And Your faithfulness by night.

PSALM 92:1-2 NASB

*The loving God we serve has
immeasurable compassion and tenderness
toward each of us throughout our lives.*

— *James Dobson* —

GOD'S BLESSING
EVERYWHERE

And all these blessings shall come upon you
and overtake you, if you obey the voice
of the LORD your God. Blessed shall you be
in the city, and blessed shall you be in the field.
Blessed shall be the fruit of your womb
and the fruit of your ground and the
fruit of your cattle.... Blessed shall be your basket
and your kneading bowl. Blessed shall you be
when you come in, and blessed
shall you be when you go out....

The LORD will command the blessing on you
in your barns and in all that you undertake.
And he will bless you in the land
that the LORD your God is giving you.
The LORD will establish you as a people
holy to himself, as he has sworn to you,
if you keep the commandments of
the LORD your God and walk in his ways....

And the LORD will make you abound
in prosperity.... The LORD will open to you
his good treasury, the heavens,
to give the rain to your land
in its season and to bless
all the work of your hands.

DEUTERONOMY 28:2-6, 8-9, 11-12 ESV

This is my Father's world;
He shines in all that's fair.
In the rustling grass
I hear Him pass;
He speaks to me everywhere.

— *Maltbie D. Babcock* —

WATCHING OVER YOU

I lift up my eyes to the mountains—
where does my help come from?
My help comes from the LORD,
the Maker of heaven and earth.
He will not let your foot slip—
he who watches over you will not slumber;
indeed, he who watches over Israel
will neither slumber nor sleep.
The LORD watches over you—
the LORD is your shade at your right hand;
the sun will not harm you by day,
nor the moon by night.
The LORD will keep you from all harm—
he will watch over your life;
the LORD will watch over your coming and going
both now and forevermore.

PSALM 121:1-8 NIV

If you make the LORD your refuge,

if you make the Most High your shelter,

no evil will conquer you;

no plague will come near your home.

For he will order his angels

to protect you wherever you go.

PSALM 91:9-11 NLT

I will counsel you with My eye upon you.

PSALM 32:8 NASB

God is constantly taking knowledge of me in love and watching over me for my good.

— *J. I. Packer* —

MARVELOUS LOVINGKINDNESS

I trust in you, LORD;

I say, "You are my God."

My times are in your hands....

Let your face shine on your servant;

save me in your unfailing love.

Let me not be put to shame, LORD,

for I have cried out to you....

How abundant are the good things

that you have stored up for those who fear you,

that you bestow in the sight of all,

on those who take refuge in you.

In the shelter of your presence you hide them

from all human intrigues;

you keep them safe in your dwelling....

Praise be to the LORD,

for he showed me the wonders of his love.

PSALM 31:14-17, 19-21 NIV

Deep calls to deep at the
sound of Your waterfalls;
All Your breakers and Your waves
have rolled over me.
The LORD will command His
lovingkindness in the daytime;
And His song will be with me in the night,
A prayer to the God of my life.

PSALM 42:7-8 NASB

Herein is grace and graciousness!
Herein is love and lovingkindness!
How it opens to us the compassion of
Jesus—so gentle, tender, considerate!

— *Charles H. Spurgeon* —

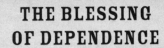

THE BLESSING
OF DEPENDENCE

You're blessed when you're at the
end of your rope. With less of you
there is more of God and his rule.

You're blessed when you feel you've lost
what is most dear to you. Only then can you be
embraced by the One most dear to you.

You're blessed when you're content with just
who you are—no more, no less. That's
the moment you find yourselves proud owners
of everything that can't be bought.

You're blessed when you've worked up
a good appetite for God. He's food and drink
in the best meal you'll ever eat.

You're blessed when you care. At the moment of
being "care-full," you find yourselves cared for.

MATTHEW 5:3-7 MSG

I pray that God, the source of hope,

will fill you completely with joy and peace

because you trust in him.

Then you will overflow with confident hope

through the power of the Holy Spirit....

And now may God, who gives us his peace,

be with you all. Amen.

ROMANS 15:13, 33 NLT

The more we
depend on God
the more dependable
we find He is.

— Cliff Richard —

LEADING, TEACHING, GUIDING

Show me the right path, O LORD;

point out the road for me to follow.

Lead me by your truth and teach me,

for you are the God who saves me.

All day long I put my hope in you.

Remember, O LORD,

your compassion and unfailing love,

which you have shown from long ages past....

The LORD is good and does what is right;

he shows the proper path to those who go astray.

He leads the humble in doing right,

teaching them his way.

PSALM 25:4-6, 8-9 NLT

In your unfailing love you will lead the people

you have redeemed. In your strength you will

guide them to your holy dwelling.

EXODUS 15:13 NIV

I'll take the hand of those who don't know the
way, who can't see where they're going.
I'll be a personal guide to them, directing them
through unknown country. I'll be right there
to show them what roads to take, make sure
they don't fall into the ditch. These are the things
I'll be doing for them—sticking with them,
not leaving them for a minute.

ISAIAH 42:16 MSG

The Lord is able to guide.
The promises cover every
imaginable situation....
Take the hand He stretches out.

— *Elisabeth Elliot* —

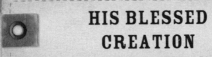

HIS BLESSED CREATION

In the beginning God created the heavens and
the earth. Now the earth was formless and empty,
darkness was over the surface of the deep, and
the Spirit of God was hovering over the waters....

So God created mankind in his own image,
in the image of God he created them;
male and female he created them.

God blessed them and said to them,
"Be fruitful and increase in number; fill the earth
and subdue it. Rule over the fish in the sea and
the birds in the sky and over every living creature
that moves on the ground."

Then God said, "I give you every seed-bearing
plant on the face of the whole earth and every
tree that has fruit with seed in it. They will be
yours for food. And to all the beasts of the earth

and all the birds in the sky and all the creatures
that move along the ground—everything
that has the breath of life in it—I give every
green plant for food." And it was so.

God saw all that he had made, and it
was very good. And there was evening,
and there was morning—the sixth day.

GENESIS 1:1-2, 27-31 NIV

*God has a wonderful plan for each
person He has chosen. He knew even
before He created this world what beauty
He would bring forth from our lives.*

— *Louise B. Wyly* —

17

ENCOURAGEMENT AND PROVISION

May the LORD answer you when you are in distress;
may the name of the God of Jacob protect you.
May he send you help from the sanctuary
and grant you support from Zion....
May he give you the desire of your heart
and make all your plans succeed.
May we shout for joy over your victory
and lift up our banners in the name of our God.
May the LORD grant all your requests.

PSALM 20:1-2, 4-5 NIV

"You are my place of safety and protection.
You are my God and I trust you."
God will save you....
He will cover you with his feathers,
and under his wings you can hide.

PSALM 91:2-4 NCV

For you are my hiding place;

you protect me from trouble.

You surround me with songs of victory.

PSALM 32:7 NLT

He is the Source. Of everything.

Strength for your day. Wisdom for

your task. Comfort for your soul.

Grace for your battle.

Provision for each need.

Understanding for each failure.

Assistance for every encounter.

— *Jack Hayford* —

DELIGHT
IN THE LORD

How blessed is the man who does not walk

in the counsel of the wicked,

Nor stand in the path of sinners,

Nor sit in the seat of scoffers!

But his delight is in the law of the LORD,

And in His law he meditates day and night.

He will be like a tree firmly planted

by streams of water,

Which yields its fruit in its season...

And in whatever he does, he prospers.

PSALM 1:1-3 NASB

The Lord makes firm the steps

of the one who delights in him;

though he may stumble, he will not fall,

for the Lord upholds him with his hand.

PSALM 37:23-24 NIV

Trust in the LORD and do good;
Dwell in the land and cultivate faithfulness.
Delight yourself in the LORD;
And He will give you the desires of your heart.
Commit your way to the LORD,
Trust also in Him, and He will do it.

PSALM 37:3-5 NASB

*God's quest to be glorified and
our quest to be satisfied reach
their goal in this one experience:
our delight in God
which overflows in praise.*

— *John Piper* —

BLESSING
ALONG THE WAY

Blessed are those whose way is blameless,
who walk in the law of the LORD!
Blessed are those who keep his testimonies,
who seek him with their whole heart....
You have commanded your precepts
to be kept diligently.
Oh that my ways may be steadfast
in keeping your statutes!
Then I shall not be put to shame,
having my eyes fixed on all your commandments.
I will praise you with an upright heart,
when I learn your righteous rules....
With my whole heart I seek you;
let me not wander from your commandments!
I have stored up your word in my heart,
that I might not sin against you.
Blessed are you, O LORD;
teach me your statutes!...

In the way of your testimonies I delight
as much as in all riches.
I will meditate on your precepts
and fix my eyes on your ways.
I will delight in your statutes;
I will not forget your word.

PSALM 119:1-2, 4-7, 10-12, 14-16 ESV

God will find us, bless us,
even when we feel most alone, unsure....
God will find a way to let us know
that He is with us in this place,
wherever we are.

— *Kathleen Norris* —

GRACE AND PEACE

May God give you more and more grace and
peace as you grow in your knowledge of God and
Jesus our Lord. By his divine power,
God has given us everything we need for
living a godly life. We have received
all of this by coming to know him,
the one who called us to himself by means
of his marvelous glory and excellence.
And because of his glory and excellence,
he has given us great and precious promises.

2 PETER 1:2-4 NLT

Grace to you and peace
from God our Father
and the Lord Jesus Christ.

ROMANS 1:7 NASB

Grace to you and peace from God our Father
and the Lord Jesus Christ. Blessed be
the God and Father of our Lord Jesus Christ,
the Father of mercies and God of all comfort,
who comforts us in all our affliction so that
we will be able to comfort those who are in
any affliction with the comfort with which we
ourselves are comforted by God.

2 CORINTHIANS 1:2-4 NASB

Among our treasures are such
wonderful things as the
grace of Christ, the love of Christ,
the joy and peace of Christ.

— *L. B. Cowman* —

CALL HER BLESSED

A wife of noble character who can find?
She is worth far more than rubies.
Her husband has full confidence in her
and lacks nothing of value.
She brings him good, not harm,
all the days of her life....

She is clothed with strength and dignity;
she can laugh at the days to come.
She speaks with wisdom,
and faithful instruction is on her tongue.
She watches over the affairs of her household
and does not eat the bread of idleness.
Her children arise and call her blessed;
her husband also, and he praises her:
"Many women do noble things,
but you surpass them all."

Charm is deceptive, and beauty is fleeting;
but a woman who fears the LORD is to be praised.
Honor her for all that her hands have done,
and let her works bring her praise at the city gate.

PROVERBS 31:10-12, 25-31 NIV

The LORD God said, "It is not good for the man to
be alone. I will make a helper suitable for him."

GENESIS 2:18 NIV

*I long to accomplish a great and
noble task, but it is my chief duty to
accomplish humble tasks as though
they were great and noble.*

— *Helen Keller* —

27

EVERY GOOD GIFT

I said to the LORD, "You are my Master!
Every good thing I have comes from you."...
LORD, you alone are my inheritance,
my cup of blessing.
You guard all that is mine....
I will bless the LORD who guides me;
even at night my heart instructs me.
I know the LORD is always with me.
I will not be shaken, for he is right beside me.
No wonder my heart is glad, and I rejoice.
My body rests in safety....
You will show me the way of life,
granting me the joy of your presence
and the pleasures of living with you forever.

PSALM 16:2, 5, 7-9, 11 NLT

If you then, being evil, know how to give
good gifts to your children, how much more

will your heavenly Father give the Holy Spirit
to those who ask Him?

LUKE 11:13 NASB

Every good and perfect gift is from above,
coming down from the Father of the heavenly
lights, who does not change like shifting shadows.

JAMES 1:17 NIV

*The life we have been given can't be
bought or bargained for. It is a gift....
If our day is indeed a gift from God,
something of the Giver should be
evident within the gift.*

— Ken Gire —

29

THE BLESSING
OF KNOWING GOD

I have not stopped giving thanks for you,
remembering you in my prayers. I keep asking
that the God of our Lord Jesus Christ,
the glorious Father, may give you the Spirit
of wisdom and revelation, so that you may
know him better. I pray that the eyes of your
heart may be enlightened in order that you may
know the hope to which he has called you,
the riches of his glorious inheritance in his
holy people, and his incomparably great power
for us who believe. That power is the same as the
mighty strength he exerted when he raised Christ
from the dead and seated him at his right hand in
the heavenly realms, far above all rule
and authority, power and dominion,
and every name that is invoked, not only in
the present age but also in the one to come.

EPHESIANS 1:16–21 NIV

If you brag, brag of this and this only:
That you understand and know me.
I'm God, and I act in loyal love.
I do what's right and set things
right and fair, and delight
in those who do the same things.

JEREMIAH 9:24 MSG

*The greatest honor
we can give God
is to live gladly
because of the knowledge
of His love.*

— *Julian of Norwich* —

FAITHFULNESS
EXTENDED

Remember your promise to me;

it is my only hope.

Your promise revives me;

it comforts me in all my troubles....

I meditate on your age-old regulations;

O LORD, they comfort me....

Your decrees have been the theme of my songs

wherever I have lived.

I reflect at night on who you are, O LORD;

therefore, I obey your instructions....

Your eternal word, O LORD,

stands firm in heaven.

Your faithfulness extends to every generation,

as enduring as the earth you created.

Your regulations remain true to this day,

for everything serves your plans.

PSALM 119:49-50, 52, 54-55, 89-91 NLT

Your steadfast love, O Lord,
extends to the heavens,
your faithfulness to the clouds.

PSALM 36:5 ESV

Peace be with you...and may God
the Father and the Lord Jesus Christ
give you love with faithfulness.

EPHESIANS 6:23-24 NLT

*Tell of His wondrous faithfulness,
and sound His power abroad;
sing the sweet promise of His grace,
the love and truth of God.*

— Isaac Watts —

THE BLESSING
OF REST

Remember the Sabbath day, to keep it holy.
Six days you shall labor,
and do all your work, but the seventh day
is a Sabbath to the LORD your God.
On it you shall not do any work,
you, or your son, or your daughter,
your male servant, or your female servant,
or your livestock, or the sojourner
who is within your gates. For in six days
the LORD made heaven and earth,
the sea, and all that is in them,
and rested on the seventh day.
Therefore the LORD blessed
the Sabbath day and made it holy.

EXODUS 20:8-11 ESV

Are you tired? Worn out?

Burned out on religion? Come to me.

Get away with me and you'll recover your life.

I'll show you how to take a real rest. Walk

with me and work with me—watch how I do it.

Learn the unforced rhythms of grace.

I won't lay anything heavy or ill-fitting on you.

Keep company with me and you'll learn

to live freely and lightly.

MATTHEW 11:28-30 MSG

Today, Lord, bless this place and time
that I've set aside to be with You.

— *Patricia Lorenz* —

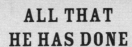

ALL THAT
HE HAS DONE

Bless the LORD, O my soul,

And forget none of His benefits;

Who pardons all your iniquities,

Who heals all your diseases;

Who redeems your life from the pit,

Who crowns you with

lovingkindness and compassion;

Who satisfies your years with good things,

So that your youth is renewed like the eagle....

The LORD is compassionate and gracious,

Slow to anger and abounding in lovingkindness....

For as high as the heavens are above the earth,

So great is His lovingkindness

toward those who fear Him.

As far as the east is from the west,

So far has He removed

our transgressions from us.

PSALM 103:2-5, 8, 11-12 NASB

Our days on earth are like grass;
like wildflowers, we bloom and die.
The wind blows, and we are gone—
as though we had never been here.
But the love of the LORD remains forever
with those who fear him.

PSALM 103:15–17 NLT

*Spend some time
walking in the workshop of the heavens,
seeing what God has done,
and watch how
your prayers are energized.*

— *Max Lucado* —

THE BLESSING
OF HARMONY

May God who gives patience, steadiness,
and encouragement help you to live in complete
harmony with each other—each with the attitude
of Christ toward the other. And then all of us can
praise the Lord together with one voice, giving
glory to God, the Father of our Lord
Jesus Christ. So, warmly welcome each other...
just as Christ has warmly welcomed you;
then God will be glorified.

ROMANS 15:5-7 TLB

Encourage one other, be of one mind,
live in peace. And the God of love and peace
will be with you.... May the grace of the Lord
Jesus Christ, and the love of God, and the
fellowship of the Holy Spirit be with you all.

2 CORINTHIANS 13:11, 14 NIV

I appeal to you, dear brothers and sisters,
by the authority of our Lord Jesus Christ,
to live in harmony with each other....
Be of one mind, united in thought and purpose.

1 CORINTHIANS 1:10 NLT

How good and pleasant it is
when God's people live together in unity!

PSALM 133:1 NIV

Nothing can give you quite the same thrill as the feeling that you are in harmony with the great God of the universe who created all things.

— *James Dobson* —

GREAT IS
YOUR GOODNESS

All your works will praise you, LORD;
your faithful people extol you.
They tell of the glory of your kingdom
and speak of your might,
so that all people may know of your mighty acts
and the glorious splendor of your kingdom.
Your kingdom is an everlasting kingdom,
and your dominion endures
through all generations.
The LORD is trustworthy in all he promises
and faithful in all he does.

PSALM 145:10-13 NIV

GOD made my life complete when I placed
all the pieces before him. When I got my
act together, he gave me a fresh start. Now I'm
alert to GOD's ways; I don't take God for granted.
Every day I review the ways he works;

I try not to miss a trick. I feel put back together,
and I'm watching my step. God rewrote
the text of my life when I opened the
book of my heart to his eyes. The good people
taste your goodness, The whole people taste
your health, The true people taste your truth.

PSALM 18:20-26 MSG

*All that is good, all that is true,
all that is beautiful, all that is
beneficent, be it great or small,
be it perfect or fragmentary, natural as
well as supernatural, moral as well
as material, comes from God.*

— John Henry Newman —

A BLESSING TO GIVE

Live generously.... Ask yourself what
you want people to do for you;
then grab the initiative and do it for them!
If you only love the lovable, do you expect a
pat on the back?... I tell you, love your enemies.
Help and give without expecting a return.
You'll never—I promise—regret it.
Live out this God-created identity
the way our Father lives toward us,
generously and graciously.

LUKE 6:30-33, 35 MSG

Give generously...and do so without
a grudging heart; then because of this
the LORD your God will bless you
in all your work and
in everything you put your hand to.

DEUTERONOMY 15:10 NIV

Give, and it will be given to you. A good measure,
pressed down, shaken together and running over,
will be poured into your lap. For with the
measure you use, it will be measured to you.

LUKE 6:38 NIV

The person who has the power to give a blessing
is greater than the one who is blessed.

HEBREWS 7:7 NLT

*To love by freely giving is its
own reward. To be possessed by love
and to in turn give love away is to
find the secret of abundant life.*

— Gloria Gaither —

FAVOR
FOR A LIFETIME

Sing the praises of the LORD....

For his anger lasts only a moment,

but his favor lasts a lifetime;

weeping may stay for the night,

but rejoicing comes in the morning.

PSALM 30:4-5 NIV

Moses said to the LORD, "You have...said, 'I know
you by name and you have found favor with me.'
If you are pleased with me, teach me your ways
so I may know you and continue to find favor
with you...." The LORD replied, "My Presence
will go with you, and I will give you rest."

EXODUS 33:12-14 NIV

The Spirit of the Lord GOD is upon me...
he has sent me to bind up the brokenhearted,
to proclaim liberty to the captives,

and the opening of the prison
to those who are bound;
to proclaim the year of the LORD's favor....
To grant to those who mourn in Zion—
to give them a beautiful headdress
instead of ashes,
the oil of gladness instead of mourning,
the garment of praise instead of a faint spirit;
that they may be called oaks of righteousness,
the planting of the LORD, that he may be glorified.

ISAIAH 61:1-3 ESV

*God longs to give favor—that is,
spiritual strength and health—to those
who seek Him, and Him alone.*

— *Teresa of Avila* —

KNOW GOD'S BLESSING

Praise the LORD!
I will thank the LORD with all my heart
as I meet with his godly people.
How amazing are the deeds of the LORD!
All who delight in him should ponder them.
Everything he does reveals his glory and majesty.
His righteousness never fails.
He causes us to remember his wonderful works.
How gracious and merciful is our LORD!
He gives food to those who fear him;
he always remembers his covenant.
He has shown his great power to his people....
All he does is just and good,
and all his commandments are trustworthy.
He has paid a full ransom for his people.
He has guaranteed his covenant
with them forever.
What a holy, awe-inspiring name he has!

Fear of the Lord is the
foundation of true wisdom.
All who obey his commandments
will grow in wisdom.

PSALM 111:1-7, 9-10 NLT

Blessed be the Lord—
day after day he carries us along.

PSALM 68:19 MSG

*The celestial order and beauty of the
universe compel me to admit that there
is some excellent and eternal Being who
deserves the respect and homage of men.*

— *Cicero* —

FRESH HOPE

GOD....rekindles burned-out lives
with fresh hope, restoring dignity and
respect to their lives—
a place in the sun! For the very structures
of earth are GOD's; he has laid out
his operations on a firm foundation.

1 SAMUEL 2:7-8 MSG

The eyes of the LORD are on those who fear him,
on those whose hope is in his unfailing love....
We wait in hope for the LORD;
he is our help and our shield.
In him our hearts rejoice,
for we trust in his holy name.
May your unfailing love be with us, LORD,
even as we put our hope in you.

PSALM 33:18, 20-22 NIV

48

You are my hope; O Lord God,

You are my confidence from my youth.

By You I have been sustained from my birth;

You are He who took me from my mother's

womb; My praise is continually of You.

PSALM 71:5-6 NASB

*God specializes in things fresh
and firsthand.... His plans for you
this year may outshine those
of the past.... He's prepared
to fill your days with reasons
to give Him praise.*

— *Joni Eareckson Tada* —

PEACE AND BLESSING

Be in agreement, understanding each other,
loving each other as family, being kind
and humble. Do not do wrong to repay a wrong,
and do not insult to repay an insult. But repay
with a blessing, because you yourselves were
called to do this so that you might receive
a blessing. The Scripture says,

"A person must do these things
to enjoy life and have many happy days....
He must stop doing evil and do good.
He must look for peace and work for it.
The Lord sees the good people
and listens to their prayers...."

If you are trying hard to do good, no one can
really hurt you. But even if you suffer
for doing right, you are blessed.

1 PETER 3:8-14 NCV

Bless those who persecute you;
bless and do not curse.
Rejoice with those who rejoice;
mourn with those who mourn.
Live in harmony with one another....
If it is possible, as far as it depends on you,
live at peace with everyone.

ROMANS 12:14–16, 18 NIV

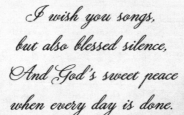

I wish you songs,
but also blessed silence,
And God's sweet peace
when every day is done.

— *Dorothy Nell McDonald* —

51

TRAVELING COMPANIONS

How blessed all those in whom you live,

whose lives become roads you travel;

They wind through lonesome valleys,

come upon brooks,

discover cool springs and pools

brimming with rain!

God-traveled, these roads

curve up the mountain, and

at the last turn—Zion! God in full view!

PSALM 84:5-7 MSG

A day in your courts is better than

a thousand elsewhere. I would rather

be a doorkeeper in the house of my God

than dwell in the tents of wickedness.

For the LORD God is a sun and shield;

the LORD bestows favor and honor.

No good thing does he withhold from those

who walk uprightly. O Lord of hosts,
blessed is the one who trusts in you!

PSALM 84:10-12 ESV

I'm still in your presence,
but you've taken my hand.
You wisely and tenderly lead me,
and then you bless me.

PSALM 73:23-24 MSG

*It is God to whom and with whom
we travel, and while He is
the End of our journey, He is also
at every stopping place.*

— Elisabeth Elliot —

BLESSINGS TO EMPOWER

When I think of all this, I fall
to my knees and pray to the Father,
the Creator of everything in heaven
and on earth. I pray that
from his glorious, unlimited resources
he will empower you with inner strength
through his Spirit. Then Christ will
make his home in your hearts
as you trust in him. Your roots will
grow down into God's love and
keep you strong. And may you have
the power to understand, as all God's
people should, how wide, how long, how high,
and how deep his love is. May you experience
the love of Christ, though it is too great
to understand fully. Then you will be made
complete with all the fullness of life
and power that comes from God.

Now all glory to God, who is able,
through his mighty power at work within us,
to accomplish infinitely more than
we might ask or think. Glory to him
in the church and in Christ Jesus through all
generations forever and ever! Amen.

EPHESIANS 3:14-21 NLT

*God often calls us to do things
that we do not have the ability to do.
Spiritual discernment is knowing if
God calls you to do something,
God empowers you to do it.*

— Suzanne Farnham —

THE ABILITY
TO BE FAITHFUL

For this very reason, make every effort to
add to your faith goodness; and to goodness,
knowledge; and to knowledge, self-control; and to
self-control, perseverance; and to perseverance,
godliness; and to godliness, mutual affection; and
to mutual affection, love. For if you possess these
qualities in increasing measure, they will keep
you from being ineffective and unproductive in
your knowledge of our Lord Jesus Christ.

2 PETER 1:5-8 NIV

We are many parts of one body, and we all belong
to each other. In his grace, God has given us
different gifts for doing certain things well. So...
if your gift is serving others, serve them well.
If you are a teacher, teach well. If your gift is to
encourage others, be encouraging. If it is giving,
give generously. If God has given you leadership

ability, take the responsibility seriously.
And if you have a gift for showing kindness
to others, do it gladly. Don't just pretend
to love others. Really love them. Hate
what is wrong. Hold tightly to what is good.

ROMANS 12:5-9 NLT

*Not everyone possesses boundless energy
or a conspicuous talent. We are not
equally blessed with great intellect or
physical beauty or emotional strength.
But we have all been given the same
ability to be faithful.*

— *Gigi Graham Tchividjian* —

BLESSING
OF PROTECTION

You, LORD, are a shield around me,

my glory, the One who lifts my head high....

I lie down and sleep;

I wake again,

because the LORD sustains me....

From the LORD comes deliverance.

May your blessing be on your people.

PSALM 3:3, 5, 8 NIV

But let all who take refuge in you rejoice;

let them ever sing for joy,

and spread your protection over them,

that those who love your name

may exult in you. For you

bless the righteous, O LORD;

you cover him with favor as with a shield.

PSALM 5:11-12 ESV

Your righteousness is like the highest mountains,
your justice like the great deep.
You, LORD, preserve both people and animals.
How priceless is your unfailing love, O God!
People take refuge in the shadow of your wings.

PSALM 36:6-7 NIV

God wants our companionship.
He wants to have us close to Him.
He wants to be a father to us,
to shield us, to protect us,
to counsel us, and to guide us
in our way through life.

— *Billy Graham* —

May God our Father and the Lord
Jesus Christ give you grace and peace.
All praise to God, the Father of our
Lord Jesus Christ, who has blessed us
with every spiritual blessing in the heavenly
realms because we are united with Christ.
Even before he made the world,
God loved us and chose us in Christ
to be holy and without fault in his eyes.
God decided in advance to adopt us
into his own family by bringing us to
himself through Jesus Christ.
This is what he wanted to do,
and it gave him great pleasure.
So we praise God for the glorious
grace he has poured out on us who
belong to his dear Son. He is so rich in
kindness and grace that he purchased

our freedom with the blood of his Son
and forgave our sins. He has showered his
kindness on us, along with all
wisdom and understanding.

EPHESIANS 1:2-8 NLT

*We must drink deeply from the
very Source the deep calm
and peace of interior quietude and
refreshment of God, allowing the
pure water of divine grace to flow
plentifully and unceasingly from
the Source itself.*

— *Mother Teresa* —

BLESSINGS IN RESPONSE

Shout joyfully to the LORD, all the earth.

Serve the LORD with gladness;

Come before Him with joyful singing.

Know that the LORD Himself is God;

It is He who has made us, and not we ourselves;

We are His people and the sheep of His pasture.

Enter His gates with thanksgiving

And His courts with praise

Give thanks to Him, bless His name.

For the LORD is good;

His lovingkindness is everlasting

And His faithfulness to all generations.

PSALM 100:1-5 NASB

Steadfast love and faithfulness meet;

righteousness and peace kiss each other.

Faithfulness springs up from the ground,

and righteousness looks down from the sky.

Yes, the LORD will give what is good....
Righteousness will go before him
and make his footsteps a way.

PSALM 85:10-13 ESV

God is sheer being itself—Spirit. Those who
worship him must do it out of their very being,
their spirits, their true selves, in adoration.

JOHN 4:24 MSG

When our reply to God is most direct
of all, it is called adoration. Adoration
is spontaneous yearning of the heart to
worship, honor, magnify, and bless God.

— *Richard J. Foster* —

REST IN HIM

Yes, my soul, find rest in God;
my hope comes from him.
Truly he is my rock and my salvation;
he is my fortress, I will not be shaken.
My salvation and my honor depend on God;
he is my mighty rock, my refuge.
Trust in him at all times, you people;
pour out your hearts to him,
for God is our refuge.

PSALM 62:5-8 NIV

The law of the LORD is perfect,
refreshing the soul.
The statutes of the LORD are trustworthy,
making wise the simple.
The precepts of the LORD are right,
giving joy to the heart.
The commands of the LORD are radiant,

giving light to the eyes.

The fear of the LORD is pure,

enduring forever.

The decrees of the LORD are firm,

and all of them are righteous.

They are more precious than gold,

than much pure gold.

PSALM 19:7–10 NIV

When God finds a soul

that rests in Him

and is not easily moved...

to this same soul He gives

the joy of His presence.

— *Catherine of Genoa* —

65

A WARDROBE
OF BLESSINGS

Now you're dressed in a new wardrobe.

Every item of your new way of life

is custom-made by the Creator,

with his label on it.... From now on

everyone is defined by Christ,

everyone is included in Christ.

So, chosen by God for this new life of love,

dress in the wardrobe God picked out for you:

compassion, kindness, humility,

quiet strength, discipline.

Be even-tempered, content with second place,

quick to forgive an offense.

Forgive as quickly and completely as

the Master forgave you.

And regardless of what else you put on,

wear love. It's your basic,

all-purpose garment. Never be without it.

COLOSSIANS 3:10-14 MSG

So in Christ Jesus you are all children of God
through faith, for all of you who were baptized
into Christ have clothed yourselves with Christ.

GALATIANS 3:26–27 NIV

May God bless you richly and grant you
increasing freedom from all anxiety and fear.

1 PETER 1:2 TLB

*The heart is rich when it is content,
and it is always content when its desires
are fixed on God. Nothing can bring
greater happiness than doing God's will
for the love of God.*

— *Miguel Febres Cordero-Muñoz* —

THE LORD HAS BEEN GOOD

I love the LORD, for he heard my voice;

he heard my cry for mercy.

Because he turned his ear to me,

I will call on him as long as I live....

I was overcome by distress and sorrow.

Then I called on the name of the LORD....

The LORD is gracious and righteous;

our God is full of compassion.

The LORD protects the unwary;

when I was brought low, he saved me.

Return to your rest, my soul,

for the LORD has been good to you.

For you, LORD, have delivered me from death,

my eyes from tears, my feet from stumbling,

that I may walk before the LORD

in the land of the living.

PSALM 116:1-9 NIV

The Lord remembers us and will bless us....
The LORD will bless those who respect him,
from the smallest to the greatest.
May the Lord give you success,
and may he give you and your children success.
May you be blessed by the LORD,
who made heaven and earth.

PSALM 115:12-15 NCV

*The Lord's goodness surrounds us
at every moment. I walk through it
almost with difficulty, as through
thick grass and flowers.*

— *R. W. Barber* —

WHEN WE BLESS OTHERS

Each of you should give what you have decided
in your heart to give, not reluctantly or under
compulsion, for God loves a cheerful giver.
And God is able to bless you abundantly,
so that in all things at all times, having all that
you need, you will abound in every good work.
As it is written:

"They have freely scattered their gifts to the poor;
their righteousness endures forever."

Now he who supplies seed to the sower and
bread for food will also supply and increase your
store of seed and will enlarge the harvest of your
righteousness. You will be enriched in every way
so that you can be generous on every occasion,
and through us your generosity will result in
thanksgiving to God.

2 CORINTHIANS 9:7-11 NIV

Each of you has received a gift
to use to serve others. Be good servants
of God's various gifts of grace.
Anyone who speaks should speak
words from God. Anyone who serves should
serve with the strength God gives
so that in everything God
will be praised through Jesus Christ.

1 PETER 4:10-11 NCV

*People who deal with life
generously and large-heartedly
go on multiplying
relationships to the end.*

— *Arthur Christopher Benson* —

71

A GRATEFUL HEART

What shall I return to the LORD
for all his goodness to me?
I will lift up the cup of salvation
and call on the name of the LORD.
I will fulfill my vows to the LORD
in the presence of all his people.

PSALM 116:12-14 NIV

You have turned my mourning
into joyful dancing.
You have taken away my clothes of mourning
and clothed me with joy,
that I might sing praises to you and not be silent.
O LORD my God, I will give you thanks forever!

PSALM 30:11-12 NLT

I will give thanks to the LORD with all my heart;
I will tell of all Your wonders.

I will be glad and exult in You;

I will sing praise to Your name,

O Most High.

PSALM 9:1-2 NASB

To you, LORD, I call;

you are my Rock....

The LORD is my strength and my shield;

my heart trusts in him, and he helps me.

My heart leaps for joy

and with my song I praise him.

PSALM 28:1, 7 NIV

You who have given so much to me,

Give one thing more—a grateful heart.

— *George Herbert* —

BLESSED AS CHILDREN OF GOD

See what great love the Father has lavished
on us, that we should be called children of God!
And that is what we are! The reason the world
does not know us is that it did not know him.
Dear friends, now we are children of God,
and what we will be has not yet been made
known. But we know that when Christ appears,
we shall be like him, for we shall see him as he is.
All who have this hope in him purify themselves,
just as he is pure.

1 JOHN 3:1-3 NIV

For you have not received a
spirit of slavery leading to fear again,
but you have received a spirit of adoption
as sons by which we cry out, "Abba! Father!"

The Spirit Himself testifies with our spirit
that we are children of God,
and if children, heirs also, heirs of God
and fellow heirs with Christ.

ROMANS 8:15-17 NASB

*An infinite God can give all of
Himself to each of His children.
He does not distribute Himself that
each may have a part, but to each one
He gives all of Himself as fully as
if there were no others.*

— A. W. Tozer —

75

GOD IS OUR HELP

If you don't know what you're doing,
pray to the Father. He loves to help.

JAMES 1:5 MSG

In the same way, the Spirit helps us
in our weakness. We do not know what
we ought to pray for, but the Spirit himself
intercedes for us through wordless groans.
And he who searches our hearts knows
the mind of the Spirit, because the Spirit
intercedes for God's people in
accordance with the will of God.
And we know that in all things
God works for the good of those who love him,
who have been called according to his purpose.

ROMANS 8:26-28 NIV

When you pray, go away by yourself, shut the door behind you, and pray to your Father in private. Then your Father, who sees everything, will reward you.... Store your treasures in heaven, where moths and rust cannot destroy, and thieves do not break in and steal. Wherever your treasure is, there the desires of your heart will also be.

MATTHEW 6:6, 20-21 NLT

When life tumbles in and problems
overwhelm us...how reassuring it is
to know that the Spirit
makes intercession for us!

— *Hazel C. Lee* —

BLESSINGS
OVERFLOW

The LORD is my shepherd; I shall not want.

He makes me lie down in green pastures.

He leads me beside still waters.

He restores my soul.

He leads me in paths of righteousness

for his name's sake.

Even though I walk through the valley

of the shadow of death,

I will fear no evil, for you are with me;

your rod and your staff, they comfort me.

You prepare a table before me

in the presence of my enemies;

you anoint my head with oil;

my cup overflows.

Surely goodness and mercy shall follow me

all the days of my life,

and I shall dwell in the house of the LORD forever.

PSALM 23:1-6 ESV

My heart overflows with a good theme;

I address my verses to the King;

My tongue is the pen of a ready writer....

Grace is poured upon Your lips;

Therefore God has blessed You forever.

PSALM 45:1-2 NASB

Let praise flow from my lips,

for you have taught me your decrees.

PSALM 119:171 NLT

Grace is...an outpouring, a boundless... offering of God's self to us, suffering with us, overflowing with tenderness.

— *Gerald G. May* —

LOVE MUCH, LOVE WELL

I pray that your love will overflow more
and more, and that you will keep on growing in
knowledge and understanding. For I want you to
understand what really matters,
so that you may live pure and blameless lives
until the day of Christ's return.

PHILIPPIANS 1:9-10 NLT

I thank my God every time I remember you.
In all my prayers for all of you, I always pray
with joy because of your partnership in the
gospel from the first day until now,
being confident of this, that he who began
a good work in you will carry it on to completion
until the day of Christ Jesus.

PHILIPPIANS 1:3-6 NIV

Oh! Teach us to live well!

Teach us to live wisely and well!...

Surprise us with love at daybreak;

then we'll skip and dance all the day long.

PSALM 90:12, 14 MSG

Remember you are very special to God
as His precious child. He has promised
to complete the good work He has
begun in you. As you continue to
grow in Him, He will teach you
to be a blessing to others.

— *Gary Smalley and John Trent* —

THE BLESSING
OF HIS NAME

Praise the LORD! Praise,

O servants of the LORD,

praise the name of the LORD!

Blessed be the name of the LORD

from this time forth and forevermore!

From the rising of the sun to its setting,

the name of the LORD is to be praised!

The LORD is high above all nations,

and his glory above the heavens!

Who is like the LORD our God,

who is seated on high,

who looks far down

on the heavens and the earth?

He raises the poor from the dust

and lifts the needy from the ash heap,

to make them sit with princes,

with the princes of his people.

PSALM 113:1-8 ESV

Blessings on the King who comes
in the name of the LORD! Peace in heaven,
and glory in highest heaven!

LUKE 19:38 NLT

Since we are receiving a kingdom that cannot be
shaken, let us be thankful, and so worship God
acceptably with reverence and awe.

HEBREWS 12:28 NIV

*There are times when to speak is
to violate the moment...when silence
represents the highest respect.
The word for such times is reverence.*

— *Max Lucado* —

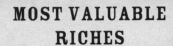

MOST VALUABLE RICHES

Let love and faithfulness never leave you;

bind them around your neck,

write them on the tablet of your heart.

Then you will win favor and a good name

in the sight of God and man.

Trust in the LORD with all your heart

and lean not on your own understanding;

in all your ways submit to him,

and he will make your paths straight....

Blessed are those who find wisdom,

those who gain understanding,

for she is more profitable than silver

and yields better returns than gold.

She is more precious than rubies;

nothing you desire can compare with her.

Long life is in her right hand;

in her left hand are riches and honor.

Her ways are pleasant ways,
and all her paths are peace.

PROVERBS 3:3-6, 13-17 NIV

Your word is a lamp to guide my feet
and a light for my path....
Your laws are my treasure;
they are my heart's delight.

PSALM 119:105, 111 NLT

*I am convinced beyond a shadow of
any doubt that the most valuable pursuit
we can embark upon is to know God.*

— *Kay Arthur* —

BLESSED IS THE NATION

May God be gracious to us and bless us
and make his face shine on us—
so that your ways may be known on earth,
your salvation among all nations.
May the peoples praise you, God;
may all the peoples praise you.
May the nations be glad and sing for joy,
for you rule the peoples with equity
and guide the nations of the earth.
May the peoples praise you, God;
may all the peoples praise you.
The land yields its harvest;
God, our God, blesses us.
May God bless us still,
So that all the ends of the earth
will fear him.

PSALM 67:1-7 NIV

The counsel of the LORD stands forever,
The plans of His heart from generation to
generation. Blessed is the nation
whose God is the LORD.

PSALM 33:11-12 NASB

*God cares for the world He created,
from the rising of a nation
to the falling of the sparrow.
Everything...lies under
the watchful gaze of
His providential eyes.*

— Ken Gire —

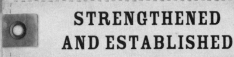

STRENGTHENED
AND ESTABLISHED

I will sing of the LORD's great love forever;

with my mouth I will make your faithfulness

known through all generations.

I will declare that your love stands firm forever,

that you have established your

faithfulness in heaven itself....

The heavens praise your wonders, LORD,

your faithfulness too,

in the assembly of the holy ones.

For who in the skies above

can compare with the LORD?

Who is like the LORD

among the heavenly beings?...

Who is like you, LORD God Almighty?

You, LORD, are mighty,

and your faithfulness surrounds you....

Blessed are those who have

learned to acclaim you,
who walk in the light of your presence, LORD.

PSALM 89:1-2, 5-6, 8, 15 NIV

The God of all grace, who called you to His
eternal glory in Christ, will Himself perfect,
confirm, strengthen and establish you.
To Him be dominion forever and ever. Amen.

1 PETER 5:10-11 NASB

*God wants His children to establish
such a close relationship with Him
that He becomes a natural partner
in all the experiences of life.*

— *Gloria Gaither* —

CONTINUOUS PRAISE

I will bless the LORD at all times;

His praise shall continually be in my mouth.

My soul will make its boast in the LORD;

The humble will hear it and rejoice.

O magnify the LORD with me,

And let us exalt His name together.

I sought the LORD, and He answered me,

And delivered me from all my fears....

The angel of the LORD encamps

around those who fear Him,

And rescues them.

O taste and see that the LORD is good;

How blessed is the man

who takes refuge in Him!

The LORD is near to the brokenhearted

And saves those who are crushed in spirit.

PSALM 34:1-4, 7-8, 18 NASB

My soul yearns, even faints,

for the courts of the LORD;

my heart and my flesh cry out

for the living God....

Blessed are those who dwell in your house;

they are ever praising you.

PSALM 84:2-4 NIV

We can go through all the activities

of our days in joyful awareness

of God's presence with whispered

prayers of praise and adoration flowing

continuously from our hearts.

— *Richard J. Foster* —

THE BLESSING
OF WORK

Neither the one who plants nor the one who
waters is anything, but only God,
who makes things grow. The one who plants and
the one who waters have one purpose, and they
will each be rewarded according to their own
labor. For we are co-workers in God's service.

1 CORINTHIANS 3:7-9 NIV

May the favor of the Lord our God rest on us;
establish the work of our hands for us —
yes, establish the work of our hands.

PSALM 90:17 NIV

From the fruit of their lips people are filled
with good things and the work
of their hands brings them reward.

PROVERBS 12:14 NIV

A faithful, sensible servant is one to whom the
master can give the responsibility of managing his
other household servants and feeding them.
If the master returns and finds that the servant
has done a good job, there will be a reward.

MATTHEW 24:45-46 NLT

*All work, from the simplest chore
to the most challenging and complex
undertaking, is a wonder and a miracle.
It is a gift and a blessing that God has
given us.... To work is to do something
essential to our humanness.*

— Ben Patterson —

HOW PRECIOUS YOUR THOUGHTS

O LORD, you have examined my heart

and know everything about me.

You know when I sit down or stand up.

You know my thoughts even when I'm far away.

You see me when I travel

and when I rest at home.

You know everything I do.

You know what I am going to say

even before I say it, LORD.

You go before me and follow me.

You place your hand of blessing on my head.

Such knowledge is too wonderful for me,

too great for me to understand!...

You saw me before I was born.

Every day of my life was recorded in your book.

Every moment was laid out

before a single day had passed.

How precious are your thoughts about me,

O God.

They cannot be numbered!
I can't even count them;
they outnumber the grains of sand!

PSALM 139:1-6, 16-18 NLT

"For my thoughts are not your thoughts,
neither are your ways my ways,"
declares the LORD. "As the heavens are
higher than the earth, so are my ways
higher than your ways and
my thoughts than your thoughts."

ISAIAH 55:8-9 NIV

*God knows the rhythm of my spirit
and knows my heart thoughts.
He is as close as breathing.*

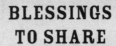
May God our Father shower you with
blessings and fill you with his great peace.
Whenever we pray for you we always
begin by giving thanks to God the Father
of our Lord Jesus Christ.... We have kept on
praying and asking God to help you
understand what he wants you to do;
asking him to make you wise about
spiritual things; and asking that the way
you live will always please the Lord
and honor him, so that you will always be
doing good, kind things for others,
while all the time you are learning to
know God better and better.
We are praying, too, that you will be filled
with his mighty, glorious strength so that
you can keep going no matter what happens—
always full of the joy of the Lord,

and always thankful to the Father
who has made us fit to share
all the wonderful things that belong to those
who live in the kingdom of light.

COLOSSIANS 1:2-3, 9-12 TLB

*Lord...give me the gift of faith to be
renewed and shared with others each day.
Teach me to live this moment only,
looking neither to the past with regret,
nor the future with apprehension.
Let love be my aim
and my life a prayer.*

— *Roseann Alexander-Isham* —

ONLY YOU

O God, You are my God;

I shall seek You earnestly;

My soul thirsts for You,

my flesh yearns for You, In a dry

and weary land where there is no water.

Thus I have seen You in the sanctuary,

To see Your power and Your glory.

Because Your lovingkindness

is better than life,

My lips will praise You.

So I will bless You as long as I live;

I will lift up my hands in Your name.

My soul is satisfied...

And my mouth offers praises with joyful lips....

I meditate on You in the night watches,

For You have been my help.

PSALM 63:1-7 NASB

Whom have I in heaven but you?

And earth has nothing I desire besides you.

My flesh and my heart may fail,

but God is the strength of my heart

and my portion forever....

It is good to be near God.

I have made the Sovereign LORD my refuge;

I will tell of all your deeds.

PSALM 73:25-26, 28 NIV

To the children of God there stands,

behind all that changes and can change,

only one unchangeable joy.

That is God.

— Hannah Whitall Smith —

THE BLESSING
OF FAITH

Since we have been made right with God
by our faith, we have peace with God.
This happened through our Lord Jesus Christ,
who through our faith has brought us into that
blessing of God's grace that we now enjoy.
And we are happy because of the hope we have
of sharing God's glory. We also have joy
with our troubles, because we know that these
troubles produce patience. And patience
produces character, and character produces hope.
And this hope will never disappoint us, because
God has poured out his love to fill our hearts.

ROMANS 5:1-5 NCV

I thank my God always when I
remember you in my prayers, because I hear
of your love and of the faith that you have toward
the Lord Jesus and for all the saints, and I pray

that the sharing of your faith may
become effective for the full knowledge
of every good thing that is in us for the
sake of Christ. For I have derived
much joy and comfort from your love...
because the hearts of the saints
have been refreshed through you.

PHILEMON 1:4-7 ESV

*When a [task] is offered to
God in faith, He blesses it
and it becomes a means not only
of serving Him in this world,
but of encountering Him here.*

— *Ben Patterson* —

IT WILL BE WELL WITH YOU

How blessed is everyone who fears the LORD,
Who walks in His ways.
When you shall eat of the fruit of your hands,
You will be happy and it will be well with you.
Your wife shall be like a fruitful vine
Within your house,
Your children like olive plants
Around your table.
Behold, for thus shall the man be blessed
Who fears the LORD.
The LORD bless you from Zion.

PSALM 128:1-5 NASB

I'm asking GOD for one thing,
only one thing:
To live with him in his house
my whole life long.
I'll contemplate his beauty;

I'll study at his feet.

That's the only quiet, secure place

in a noisy world, The perfect getaway,

far from the buzz of traffic....

Point me down your highway, GOD;

direct me along a well-lighted street....

I'm sure now I'll see God's goodness

in the exuberant earth.

PSALM 27:4-5, 11, 13 MSG

Seeing our Father in everything makes
life one long thanksgiving and gives
a rest of heart, and, more than that,
a joyfulness of spirit that is unspeakable.

— *Hannah Whitall Smith* —

FROM THE
GOOD SHEPHERD

Blessed be GOD—he heard me praying.

He proved he's on my side....

GOD is all strength for his people....

Save your people and bless your heritage.

Care for them;

carry them like a good shepherd.

PSALM 28:6, 8-9 MSG

Now may the God of peace—who brought
up from the dead our Lord Jesus, the great
Shepherd of the sheep, and ratified an eternal
covenant with his blood—may he equip you
with all you need for doing his will. May he
produce in you, through the power of Jesus
Christ, every good thing that is pleasing to him.
All glory to him forever and ever! Amen....
May God's grace be with you all.

HEBREWS 13:20-21, 25 NLT

Come, let us bow down in worship,
let us kneel before the LORD our Maker;
for he is our God
and we are the people of his pasture,
the flock under his care.

PSALM 95:6-7 NIV

When God has become our shepherd,
our refuge, our fortress,
then we can reach out to Him
in the midst of a broken world
and feel at home
while still on the way.

— *Henri J. M. Nouwen* —

HE SATISFIES

Give thanks to the LORD, for he is good;
his love endures forever.
Let the redeemed of the LORD tell their story....
They were hungry and thirsty,
and their lives ebbed away.
Then they cried out to the LORD in their trouble,
and he delivered them from their distress....
Let them give thanks to the LORD
for his unfailing love
and his wonderful deeds for mankind,
for he satisfies the thirsty
and fills the hungry with good things....
He brought them out of darkness,
the utter darkness,
and broke away their chains....
He stilled the storm to a whisper;
the waves of the sea were hushed.
They were glad when it grew calm,
and he guided them to their desired haven.

Let them give thanks to the LORD
for his unfailing love
and his wonderful deeds for mankind.

PSALM 107:1-2, 5-6, 8-9, 14, 29-31 NIV

Blessed be God,
Who has not turned away my prayer
Nor His lovingkindness from me.

PSALM 66:20 NASB

Let us, with a gladsome mind,
Praise the Lord, for He is kind:
For His mercies aye endure,
Ever faithful, ever sure.

— *John Milton* —

BLESSINGS
FOR A FAMILY

This is what the LORD says....
I will pour out my Spirit on your offspring,
and my blessing on your descendants.
They will spring up like grass in a meadow,
like poplar trees by flowing streams.

ISAIAH 44:2-4 NIV

"Let the children come to me. Don't stop them!
For the Kingdom of God belongs to those who
are like these children. I tell you the truth,
anyone who doesn't receive the Kingdom of God
like a child will never enter it." Then he took
the children in his arms and placed his hands
on their heads and blessed them.

MARK 10:14-16 NLT

So now you...are no longer strangers
and foreigners. You are citizens along
with all of God's holy people. You are
members of God's family. Together,
we are his house, built on the foundation
of the apostles and the prophets.
And the cornerstone is Christ Jesus himself.

EPHESIANS 2:19-20 NLT

*Having someone who understands you
is home. Having someone
who loves you is belonging.
Having both is a blessing.*

GIVE YOURSELF TO GOD

Blessed is the man who makes
the LORD his trust,
who does not turn to the proud,
to those who go astray after a lie!
You have multiplied, O LORD my God,
your wondrous deeds
and your thoughts toward us;
none can compare with you!
I will proclaim and tell of them,
yet they are more than can be told.

PSALM 40:4-5 ESV

I urge you...in view of God's mercy, to offer
your bodies as a living sacrifice, holy and pleasing
to God—this is your true and proper worship.
Do not conform to the pattern of this world,
but be transformed by the renewing of your mind.

ROMANS 12:1-2 NIV

Now may the God of peace make you
holy in every way, and may your whole spirit and
soul and body be kept blameless until
our Lord Jesus Christ comes again.
God will make this happen, for he who
calls you is faithful.... May the grace of our Lord
Jesus Christ be with you.

1 THESSALONIANS 5:23-24, 28 NLT

Let us give all that lies within us...
to pure praise, to pure loving adoration,
and to worship from a grateful heart—
a heart that is trained to look up.

— *Amy Carmichael* —

HIS PROMISES
PROVE TRUE

I love you, LORD, my strength.

The LORD is my rock, my fortress

and my deliverer;

my God is my rock, in whom I take refuge,

my shield and the horn of my salvation,

my stronghold....

In my distress I called to the LORD;

I cried to my God for help.

From his temple he heard my voice;

my cry came before him, into his ears....

He reached down from on high

and took hold of me;

he drew me out of deep waters....

He brought me out into a spacious place;

he rescued me because he delighted in me....

You, LORD, keep my lamp burning;

my God turns my darkness into light....

As for God, his way is perfect:

The LORD's word is flawless;

he shields all who take refuge in him.

For who is God besides the LORD?

And who is the Rock except our God?

It is God who arms me with strength

and keeps my way secure.

PSALM 18:1-2, 6, 16, 19, 28, 30-32 NIV

God takes care of His own....
He stands ready to come to our rescue.
And at just the right moment He
steps in and proves Himself as our
faithful heavenly Father.

— *Charles Swindoll* —

A BLESSING
TO SERVE

Dear brothers and sisters, we can't help
but thank God for you, because your faith
is flourishing and your love for one another
is growing.... We keep on praying for you,
asking our God to enable you to live a life
worthy of his call. May he give you the power
to accomplish all the good things your faith
prompts you to do. Then the name of
our Lord Jesus will be honored because of
the way you live, and you will be honored
along with him. This is all made possible because
of the grace of our God and Lord, Jesus Christ.

2 THESSALONIANS 1:3, 11-12 NLT

A generous person will prosper;
whoever refreshes others will be refreshed.

PROVERBS 11:25 NIV

Exercise daily in God.... Workouts in the
gymnasium are useful, but a disciplined life
in God is far more so, making you fit
both today and forever. You can count on this.
Take it to heart.

1 TIMOTHY 4:7-8 MSG

*To love God, to serve Him
because we love Him, is…
our highest happiness….
Love makes all labor light.
We serve with enthusiasm
where we love with sincerity.*

— *Hannah More* —

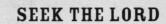

SEEK THE LORD

If God cares so wonderfully for flowers that are
here today and thrown into the fire tomorrow,
he will certainly care for you. Why do you have
so little faith? And don't be concerned about what
to eat and what to drink. Don't worry about such
things. These things dominate the thoughts of
unbelievers all over the world, but your Father
already knows your needs. Seek the Kingdom
of God above all else, and he will give you
everything you need.

LUKE 12:28-31 NLT

The God who made the world and everything
in it is the Lord of heaven and earth....
He himself gives everyone life and breath and
everything else.... God did this so that they would
seek him and perhaps reach out for him
and find him, though he is not far

from any one of us. "For in him we live,
and move, and have our being."

ACTS 17:24-25, 27-28 NIV

I love those who love me; and those who
diligently seek me will find me.

PROVERBS 8:17 NASB

God is not an elusive dream or a
phantom to chase, but a divine
person to know. He does not avoid us,
but seeks us. When we seek Him,
the contact is instantaneous.

— *Neva Coyle* —

117

ABUNDANT BLESSINGS

How blessed is the one whom
You choose and bring near to You
To dwell in Your courts.
We will be satisfied with the goodness of
Your house, Your holy temple.
By awesome deeds You answer us
in righteousness,
O God of our salvation....
They who dwell in the ends of the earth
stand in awe of Your signs;
You make the dawn and the sunset shout for joy.
You visit the earth and cause it to overflow;
You greatly enrich it;
The stream of God is full of water....
You water its furrows abundantly...
You bless its growth.
You have crowned the year with Your bounty.

PSALM 65:4-5, 8-11 NASB

And now, GOD, do it again—
bring rains to our drought-stricken lives
So those who planted their crops in despair
will shout hurrahs at the harvest,
So those who went off with heavy hearts
will come home laughing,
with armloads of blessing.

PSALM 126:4-6 MSG

*The Creator thinks enough of you
to have sent Someone very special
so that you might have life—
abundantly, joyfully, completely,
and victoriously.*

STRONG TO THE END

May God our Father and the Lord Jesus Christ
give you grace and peace. I always thank
my God for you and for the gracious gifts he has
given you.... He will keep you strong to the end
so that you will be free from all blame on the day
when our Lord Jesus Christ returns.
God will do this, for he is faithful to do
what he says, and he has invited you into
partnership with his Son, Jesus Christ our Lord.

1 CORINTHIANS 1:3-4, 8-9 NLT

Finally, be strong in the Lord and in his mighty
power.... Put on the full armor of God, so that
when the day of evil comes, you may be able to
stand your ground, and after
you have done everything, to stand.

EPHESIANS 6:10, 13 NIV

Now may our Lord Jesus Christ himself,
and God our Father, who loved us and gave us
eternal comfort and good hope through grace,
comfort your hearts and establish them in
every good work and word.

2 THESSALONIANS 2:16–17 ESV

*Taken separately, the experiences of life
can work harm and not good.
Taken together, they make a pattern
of blessing and strength
the like of which
the world does not know.*

— *V. Raymond Edman* —

MIRACLES
AND WONDERS

Oh give thanks to the LORD; call upon his name;

make known his deeds among the peoples!

Sing to him, sing praises to him;

tell of all his wondrous works!

Glory in his holy name;

let the hearts of those

who seek the LORD rejoice!

Seek the LORD and his strength;

seek his presence continually!

Remember the wondrous works that he has done,

his miracles, and the judgments he uttered....

He is the LORD our God;

his judgments are in all the earth.

He remembers his covenant forever,

the word that he commanded,

for a thousand generations.

PSALM 105:1-5, 7-8 ESV

Stop and consider the wonderful miracles of God!

Do you know how God controls the storm

and causes the lightning

to flash from his clouds?...

We cannot imagine the power of the Almighty;

but even though he is just and righteous,

he does not destroy us.

No wonder people everywhere fear him.

All who are wise show him reverence.

JOB 37:14-15, 23-24 NLT

*Miracles are nothing
other than God's advancing truth
seen with surprised eyes.*

— *Gerald G. May* —

BLESSING
AND MERCY

Blessed be the God and Father of our Lord
Jesus Christ, who according to His great mercy
has caused us to be born again to a living hope
through the resurrection of Jesus Christ.

1 PETER 1:3 NASB

Who is wise and understanding among you?
Let them show it by their good life, by deeds
done in the humility that comes from wisdom....
The wisdom that comes from heaven is
first of all pure; then peace-loving, considerate,
submissive, full of mercy and good fruit,
impartial and sincere. Peacemakers who sow
in peace reap a harvest of righteousness.

JAMES 3:13, 17-18 NIV

As you know, we count as blessed those
who have persevered. You have heard

of Job's perseverance and have seen what
the Lord finally brought about. The Lord
is full of compassion and mercy.

JAMES 5:11 NIV

Now let your unfailing love comfort me,
just as you promised me, your servant.
Surround me with your tender mercies so
I may live, for your instructions are my delight.

PSALM 119:76-77 NLT

*The quality of mercy
is not strained, It droppeth as
the gentle rain from heaven.*

— William Shakespeare —

RENEWED EVERY DAY

Though our bodies are dying, our spirits are
being renewed every day. For our present
troubles are small and won't last very long.
Yet they produce for us a glory that vastly
outweighs them and will last forever!
So we don't look at the troubles we can see now;
rather, we fix our gaze on things
that cannot be seen. For the things we see now
will soon be gone, but the things we
cannot see will last forever.

2 CORINTHIANS 4:16-18 NLT

Create in me a pure heart, O God,
and renew a steadfast spirit within me....
Restore to me the joy of your salvation
and grant me a willing spirit, to sustain me.

PSALM 51:10, 12 NIV

Now to Him who is able to keep you from
stumbling, and to make you stand in the presence
of His glory blameless with great joy, to the only
God our Savior, through Jesus Christ our Lord,
be glory, majesty, dominion and authority,
before all time and now and forever. Amen.

JUDE 1:24-25 NASB

*Be still, and in the quiet moments,
listen to the voice of your
heavenly Father. His words can
renew your spirit...no one knows you
and your needs like He does.*

— *Janet L. Weaver Smith* —

127

BLESSING
OF SALVATION

The LORD is my strength and song,

And He has become my salvation....

I shall give thanks to You,

for You have answered me,

And You have become my salvation.

The stone which the builders rejected

Has become the chief corner stone.

This is the LORD's doing;

It is marvelous in our eyes.

This is the day which the LORD has made;

Let us rejoice and be glad in it....

Blessed is the one who comes

in the name of the LORD;

We have blessed you from the house of the LORD.

The LORD is God, and He has given us light....

You are my God, and I give thanks to You;

You are my God, I extol You.

Give thanks to the LORD, for He is good;
For His lovingkindness is everlasting.

PSALM 118:14, 21-24, 26-29 NASB

This is what the LORD says:
"In the time of my favor I will answer you,
and in the day of salvation I will help you;
I will keep you and will make you
to be a covenant for the people."

ISAIAH 49:8 NIV

*Salvation comes through Him.
It is free. We can't earn salvation.
It is priceless.*

— Irene Imbler —

HIS WONDERFUL DEEDS

Sing to the LORD a new song;

Sing to the LORD, all the earth.

Sing to the LORD, bless His name;

Proclaim good tidings of His salvation

from day to day.

Tell of His glory among the nations,

His wonderful deeds among all the peoples.

For great is the LORD and greatly to be praised;

He is to be feared above all gods.

For all the gods of the peoples are idols,

But the LORD made the heavens.

Splendor and majesty are before Him,

Strength and beauty are in His sanctuary.

Ascribe to the LORD, O families of the peoples,

Ascribe to the LORD glory and strength.

Ascribe to the LORD the glory of His name;

Bring an offering and come into His courts.

Worship the LORD in holy attire;
Tremble before Him, all the earth.
Say among the nations, "The LORD reigns."

PSALM 96:1-10 NASB

*One of the most wonderful things about
knowing God is that there's always
so much more to know, so much more
to discover. Just when we
least expect it, He intrudes into our
neat and tidy notions about who
He is and how He works.*

— Joni Eareckson Tada —

BLESSING, GLORY, AND HONOR

Honor the LORD, you heavenly beings;

honor the LORD for his glory and strength.

Honor the LORD for the glory of his name.

Worship the LORD in the splendor of his holiness.

The voice of the LORD echoes above the sea.

The God of glory thunders.

The LORD thunders over the mighty sea.

The voice of the LORD is powerful;

the voice of the LORD is majestic.

The voice of the LORD splits the mighty cedars....

The voice of the LORD strikes

with bolts of lightning....

In his Temple everyone shouts, "Glory!"

The LORD rules over the floodwaters.

The LORD reigns as king forever.

The LORD gives his people strength.

The LORD blesses them with peace.

PSALM 29:1-5, 7-11 NLT

Now to the King eternal, immortal,
invisible, the only God, be honor
and glory forever and ever.

1 TIMOTHY 1:17 NASB

Amen, blessing and glory and wisdom and
thanksgiving and honor and power and might,
be to our God forever and ever. Amen.

REVELATION 7:12 NASB

*All glory and honor be unto Him
in whom are comprehended all the
blessings whereby God has enriched
His people in time and in eternity.*

— *Charles H. Spurgeon* —

YOUR PLACE
IN THE KINGDOM

You're blessed when you get your inside world—
your mind and heart—put right. Then
you can see God in the outside world.
You're blessed when you can show people
how to cooperate instead of compete or fight.
That's when you discover who you really are,
and your place in God's family.
You're blessed when your commitment to God
provokes persecution. The persecution drives you
even deeper into God's kingdom....
And all heaven applauds.

MATTHEW 5:8-10, 12 MSG

Blessed is the one who perseveres under trial
because, having stood the test, that person
will receive the crown of life that the Lord has
promised to those who love him.

JAMES 1:12 NIV

We have a priceless inheritance —
an inheritance that is kept in heaven for you,
pure and undefiled, beyond the reach of
change and decay. And through your faith,
God is protecting you by his power until you
receive this salvation, which is ready to be
revealed on the last day for all to see. So be
truly glad. There is wonderful joy ahead.

1 PETER 1:4-6 NLT

*Lift up your eyes. Your heavenly
Father waits to bless you —
in inconceivable ways to make your life
what you never dreamed it could be.*

— Anne Ortlund —

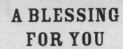

A BLESSING
FOR YOU

The LORD bless you, and keep you;

The LORD make His face shine on you,

And be gracious to you;

The LORD lift up His countenance on you,

And give you peace.

NUMBERS 6:24-26 NASB